start at the other end!

Leila's Persian Alphabet Adventure

Beginning Farsi
Activity and Coloring Workbook

Solmaz Parveen

The Persian Alphabet

الفبتای فارسی

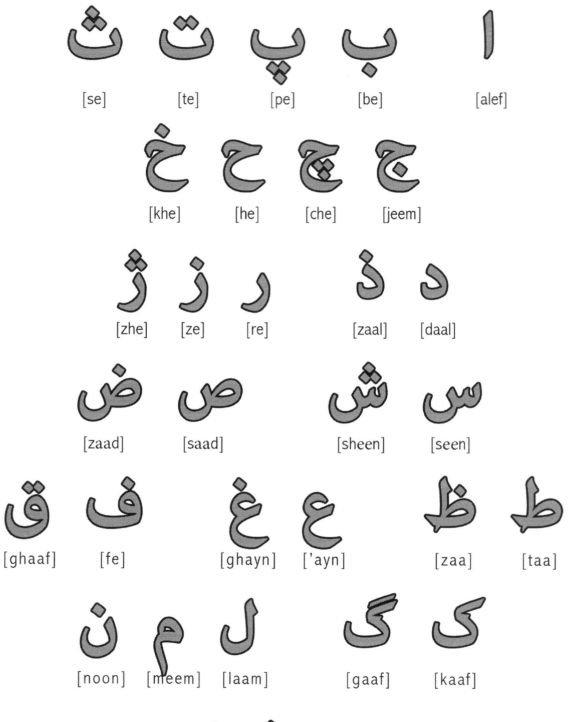

ث [se]   ت [te]   پ [pe]   ب [be]   ا [alef]

خ [khe]   ح [he]   چ [che]   ج [jeem]

ژ [zhe]   ز [ze]   ر [re]   ذ [zaal]   د [daal]

ض [zaad]   ص [saad]   ش [sheen]   س [seen]

ق [ghaaf]   ف [fe]   غ [ghayn]   ع ['ayn]   ظ [zaa]   ط [taa]

ن [noon]   م [meem]   ل [laam]   گ [gaaf]   ک [kaaf]

ی [ye]   ه [he]   و [vaav]

For Parents

Welcome to Leila's Persian Alphabet Adventure...

This book gives your child the opportunity to familiarize himself or herself with the Persian alphabet and to learn how letters are strung together to form simple words. The coloring and activity pages will help make learning fun and engaging.

First, your child will become familiar with the letters by coloring in and tracing the shapes. Dot-to-dot activities are a fun way to reinforce alphabetical order. There are also plenty of opportunities to practice writing the letters individually and in alphabetical order.

In the second half of the book, your child will see how letters join to form 50 simple words. The words in this book are not always the most common, but have been chosen for their ability to demonstrate the various forms different letters take when used in the initial, middle, or end position. Illustrations accompany the introduction of each new word. English translations, however, are purposely omitted. Children will be able to associate words with the matching object without needing to translate between languages in their heads. That said, it may be helpful to occasionally write in explanations. Finally, activity pages towards the end of the book will test your child's new knowledge.

You can help nurture your child's interest in learning the Persian alphabet and Farsi language by repeating the alphabet out loud, sounding out letters, and reading words with him or her. Maintain a relaxed environment when doing exercises, offer encouragement at the end of each activity, and try to limit practice to a few pages per day. This way alphabet and reading practice will come to an end when your child is still eager to learn more.

To begin, remove the alphabet chart from the previous page and hang it where your child will see it often to encourage memorization of the letter shapes and names. Now it's time to let your child begin coloring and drawing. And don't worry... this book features quality paper that is meant to stand up to enthusiastic coloring. Enjoy!

About Farsi/Persian Language

Farsi is the name of the Persian language in the Persian language itself. Farsi is spoken widely in Iran and Afghanistan, and in some parts of Tajikistan, Uzbekistan, Armenia, Turkmenistan, Azerbaijan, Pakistan and India.

The Persian alphabet has 32 letters. There is no capital and lowercase distinction. Each letter can have up to 4 different forms, however, depending on where it is found in a word and whether it can be connected to the letter before or after it. This book was designed for children and therefore does not contain lengthy explanations of the rules of when to use various letter forms. With repitition and guidance, they will learn how the letters take different forms.

Finally, Farsi is written from right to left. Because of this, exercises begin at the opposite end of this book.

About the Author

Solmaz Parveen is a second generation Persian American who was inspired to create the Leila's Adventures series after failing to find modern, relevant and engaging material to help her teach her own daughter about Persian culture and language.

The Leila's Adventures series covers topics from cultural holidays to basic cooking to beginning language instruction. Each book has been carefully researched and infused with modern educational philosophy. They introduce new concepts in a fun and interactive way, allowing children to master new skills and concepts easily and without anxiety or frustration. As a result, children are motivated to learn about Persian culture and language on their own.

Learn more with Leila's Adventures!

Check leilasadventures.com for more learning games, coloring sheets, and information about other Leila's Adventures books that are currently available.

English	Phonetic	Persian		English	Phonetic	Persian
sugar	[shekar]	شکر		water	[aab]	اب
shell	[sadaf]	صدف		horse	[asb]	اسب
persian drum	[zarb]	ضرب		plum	[aloo]	الو
parrot	[tootee]	طوطی		pomegranate	[anaar]	انار
container	[zarf]	ظرف		dad	[baabaa]	بابا
glasses	[aynak]	عینک		load	[baar]	بار
goose	[ghaaz]	غاز		garden	[baagh]	باغ
pepper	[felfel]	فلفل		wing	[baal]	بال
elephant	[feel]	فیل		leaf	[barg]	برگ
book	[ketaab]	کتاب		foot	[paa]	پا
bag/purse	[keef]	کیف		cheese	[paneer]	پنیر
flower	[gul]	گل		money	[pool]	پول
ear	[goosh]	گوش		instrument	[taar]	تار
lemon	[leemoo]	لیمو		ball	[toop]	توپ
snake	[maar]	مار		berry	[toot]	توت
moon	[maah]	ماه		cup	[jaam]	جام
hen	[morgh]	مرغ		chicken	[joojeh]	جوجه
eyelash	[mozheh]	مژه		tea	[chaay]	چای
mouse	[moosh]	موش		fence	[hefaaz]	حفاظ
bread	[naan]	نان		house	[khaaneh]	خانه
salt	[namak]	نمک		hand	[dast]	دست
peach	[holoo]	هلو		corn	[zorat]	ذرت
jasmin	[yaas]	یاس		basket	[sabad]	سبد
				garlic	[seer]	سیر
				dinner	[shaam]	شام
				candle	[sham']	شمع
				lion	[sheer]	شیر

Draw a line to match the words with their correct pictures.

شکر

پنیر

نان

نمک

فلفل

چای

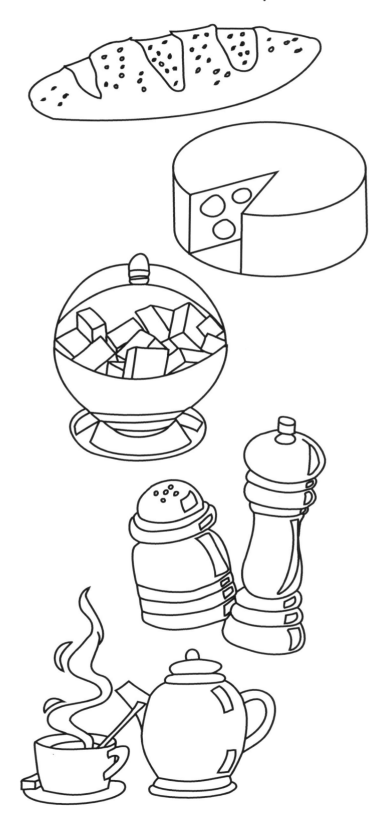

Draw a line to match the words with their correct pictures.

سیر

صدف

ماه

گل

برگ

Draw a line to match the words with their correct pictures.

پا

مژه

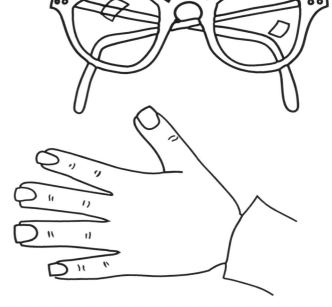

گوش

دست

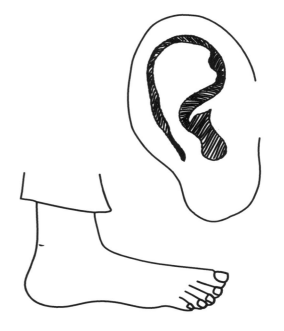

عینک

Draw a line to match the words with their correct pictures.

غاز

جوجه

موش

طوطی

Draw a line to match the words with their correct pictures.

اسب

فیل

مار

شیر

Draw a line to match the words with their correct pictures.

الو

انار

توت

سیب

لیمو

هلو

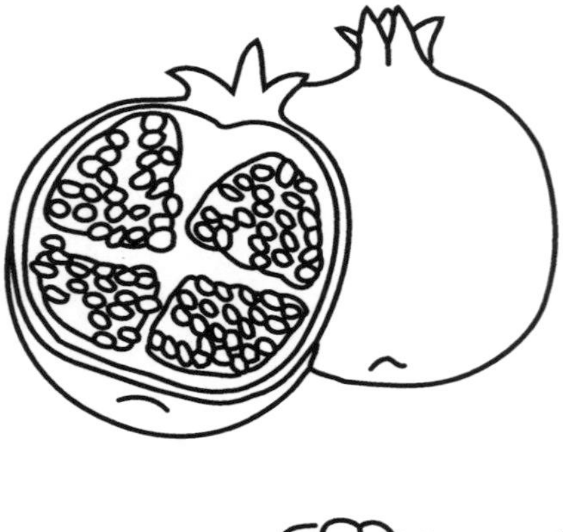

Fill in the letters that join to make each of the words below.

پنیر = _____ + _____ + _____ + _____

طوطی = _____ + _____ + _____ + _____

خانه = _____ + _____ + _____ + _____

کتاب = _____ + _____ + _____ + _____

جوجه = _____ + _____ + _____ + _____

لیمو = _____ + _____ + _____ + _____

حفاظ = _____ + _____ + _____ + _____

فلفل = _____ + _____ + _____ + _____

بابا = _____ + _____ + _____ + _____

انار = _____ + _____ + _____ + _____

عینک = _____ + _____ + _____ + _____

Fill in the letters that join to make each of the words below.

فیل = ------- + ------- + -------

شکر = ------- + ------- + -------

شام = ------- + ------- + -------

برگ = ------- + ------- + -------

مرغ = ------- + ------- + -------

نان = ------- + ------- + -------

الو = ------- + ------- + -------

توپ = ------- + ------- + -------

ماه = ------- + ------- + -------

هلو = ------- + ------- + -------

چای = ------- + ------- + -------

یاس = ------- + ------- + -------

نمک = ------- + ------- + -------

Fill in the letters that join to make each of the words below.

گَل = _____ + _____

توت = _____ + _____ + _____

تار = _____ + _____ + _____

پول = _____ + _____ + _____

سیب = _____ + _____ + _____

ظرف = _____ + _____ + _____

ضرب = _____ + _____ + _____

شیر = _____ + _____ + _____

شمع = _____ + _____ + _____

سیر = _____ + _____ + _____

صدف = _____ + _____ + _____

گوش = _____ + _____ + _____

سبد = _____ + _____ + _____

Fill in the letters that join to make each of the words below.

اب = ---------- + ----------

پا = ---------- + ----------

بار = ---------- + ---------- + ----------

موش = ---------- + ---------- + ----------

دست = ---------- + ---------- + ----------

غاز = ---------- + ---------- + ----------

مژه = ---------- + ---------- + ----------

اسب = ---------- + ---------- + ----------

مار = ---------- + ---------- + ----------

بال = ---------- + ---------- + ----------

کیف = ---------- + ---------- + ----------

باغ = ---------- + ---------- + ----------

جام = ---------- + ---------- + ----------

ح + ف + ا + ظ = حفاظ

[hefaaz]   [zaa] [alef] [fe] [he]

حفاظ

طوطى = ى + ط + و + ط

[tootee]   [ye] [taa] [vaav] [taa]

طوطى

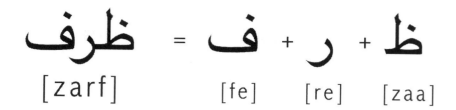

ظ + ر + ف = ظرف

[zarf]　　[fe]　[re]　[zaa]

ظرف

ض + ر + ب = ضرب

[zarb]　　　[be] [re] [zaad]

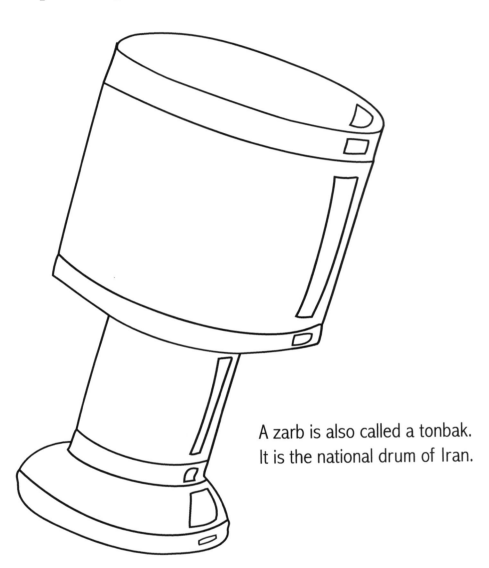

A zarb is also called a tonbak.
It is the national drum of Iran.

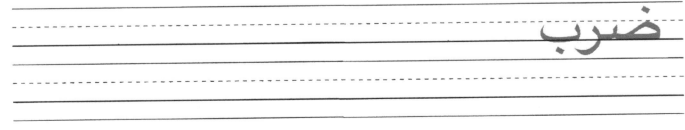

ضرب

صدف = ف + د + ص

[sadaf] [fe] [daal] [saad]

صدف

شمع = ع + م + ش

[sham'] ['ayn] [meem] [sheen]

شمع

ش + ک + ر = شکر

[shekar]   [re] [kaaf] [sheen]

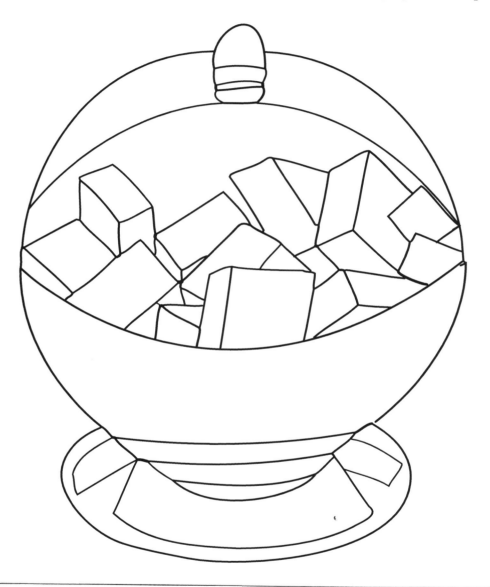

شکر

ش + ا + م = شام

[shaam]　　[meem] [alef] [sheen]

شام

سیر = ر + ی + س

[seer] [re] [ye] [seen]

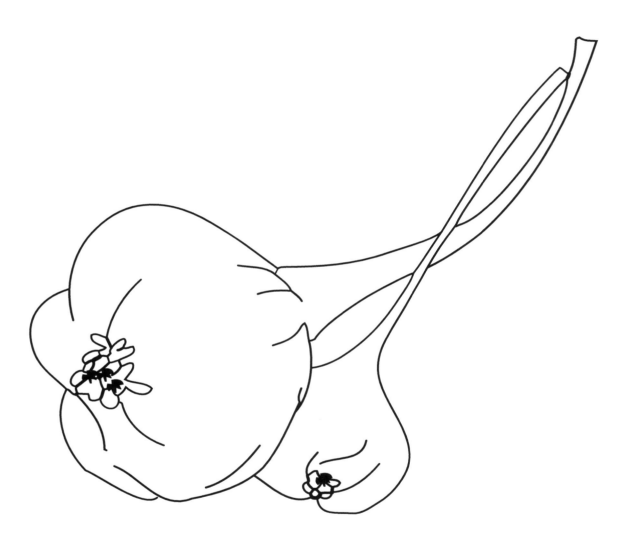

سیر

ش + ی + ر = شیر

[sheer]   [re] [ye] [sheen]

شیر

س + ب + د = سبد

[sabad] [daal] [be] [seen]

سبد

ف + ل + ف + ل = فلفل

[laam] [fe] [laam] [fe]　　[felfel]

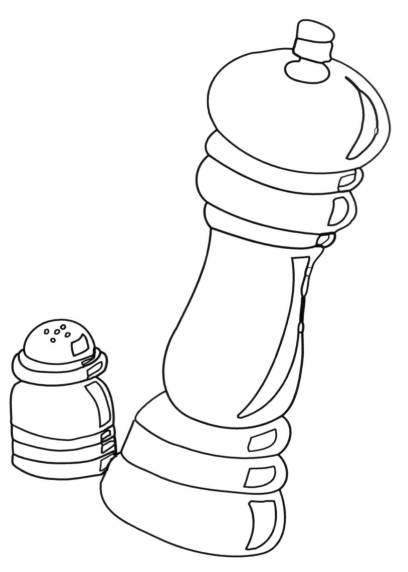

فلفل

ف + ى + ل = فيل

[fe] [ye] [laam]   [feel]

فيل

غ + ا + ز = غاز

[ghaaz]   [ze] [alef] [ghayn]

غاز

ع + ى + ن + ک = عينک

[aynak]   [kaaf] [noon] [ye] ['ayn]

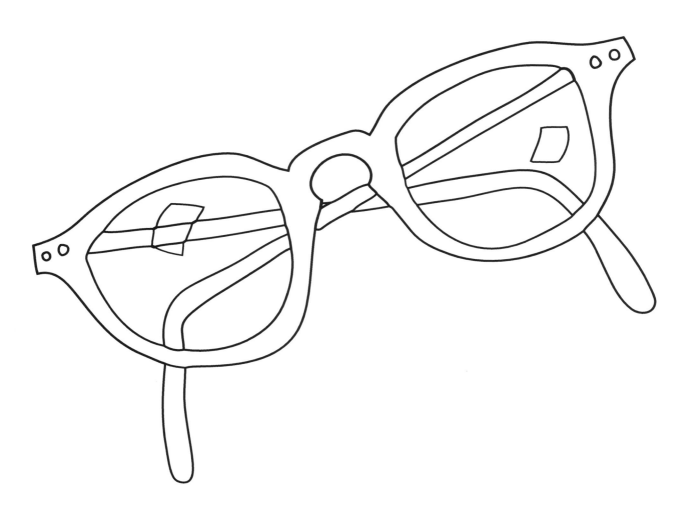

عينک

ج + و + ج + ه = جوجه

[he] [jeem] [vaav] [jeem]   [joojeh]

جوجه

خ + ا + ن + ه = خانه

[khaaneh] [he] [noon] [alef] [khe]

خانه

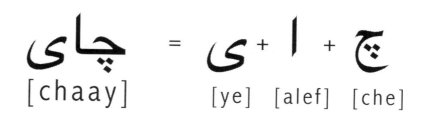

چای = ی + ا + چ
[chaay] [ye] [alef] [che]

ن + م + ک = نمک

[namak]　　[kaaf] [meem] [noon]

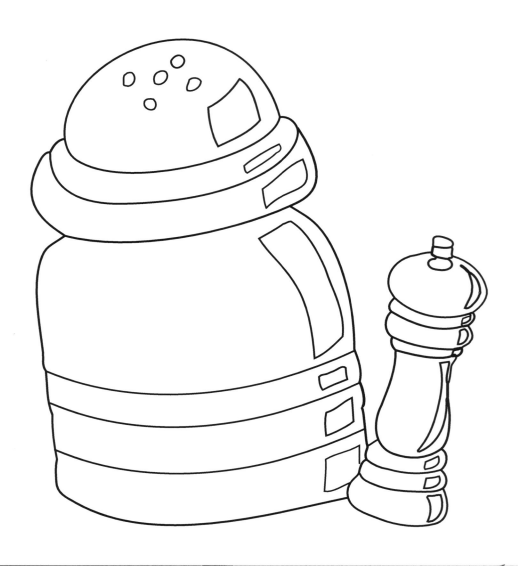

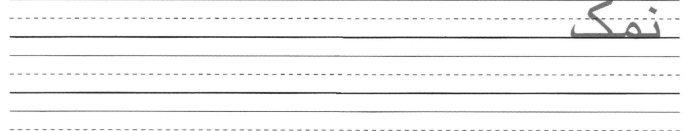

نمک

پنیر = ر + ی + ن + پ

[paneer] [re] [ye] [noon] [pe]

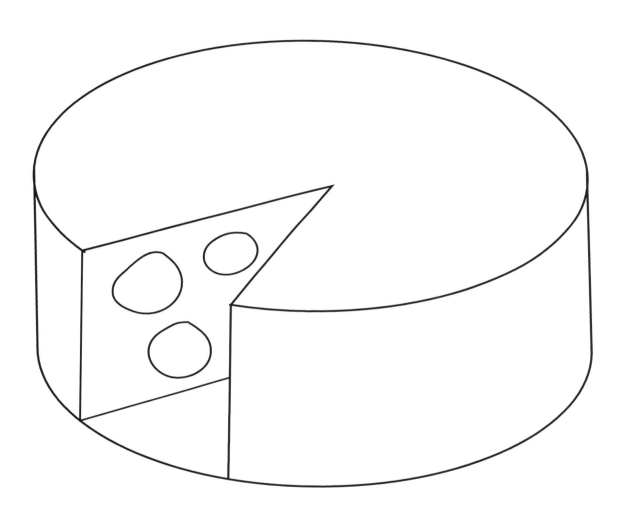

پنیر

ذ + ر + ت = ذرت

[zorat]　　[te] [re] [zaal]

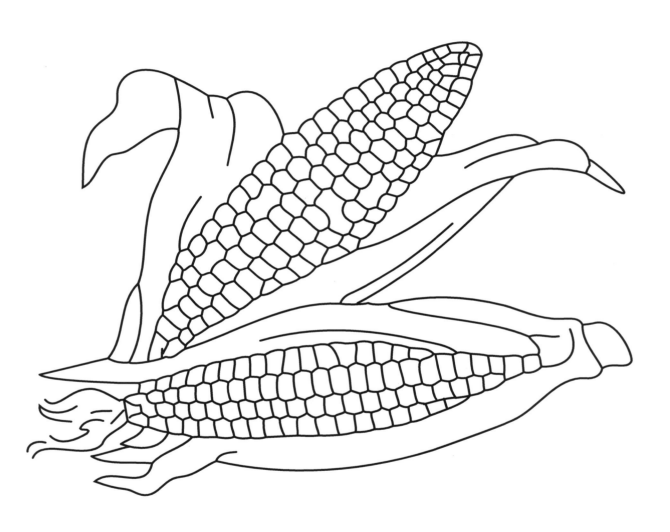

ذرت

د + س + ت = دست

[dast]   [te] [seen] [daal]

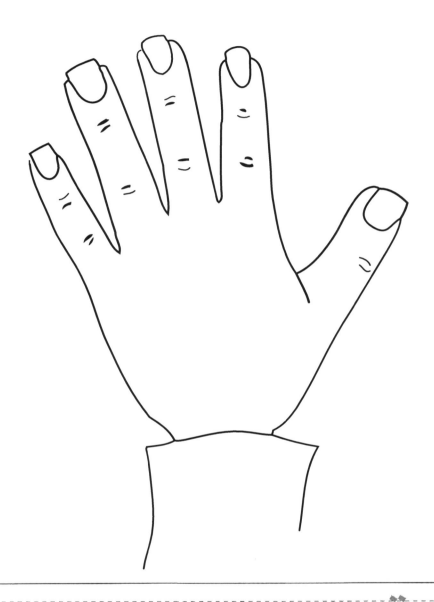

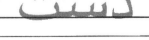

ه + ل + و = هلو

[haloo]   [vaav] [laam] [he]

هلو

م + ژ + ه = مژه
[meem] [zhe] [he]   [mozheh]

مژه

م + و + ش = موش

[moosh]   [sheen] [vaav] [meem]

موش

م + ر + غ = مرغ

[meem] [re] [ghayn] [moorgh]

مرغ

م + ا + ر = مار

[maar]   [re] [alef] [meem]

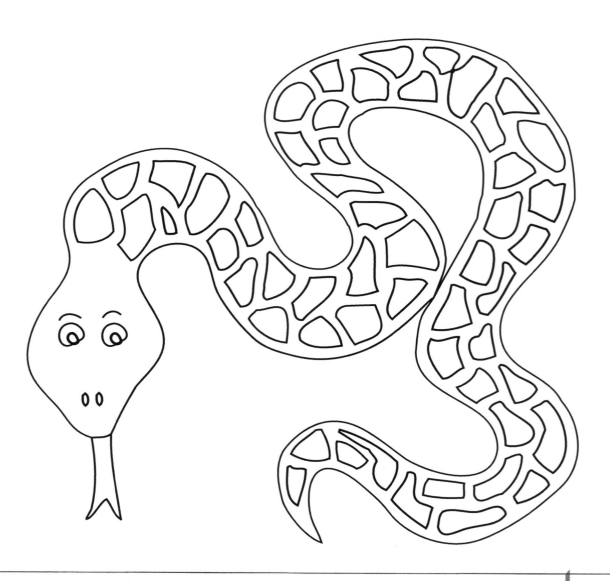

مار

م + ا + ه = ماه

[meem] [alef] [he]   [maah]

ماه

ک + ت + ا + ب = کتاب

[ketaab]   [be] [alef] [te] [kaaf]

کتاب

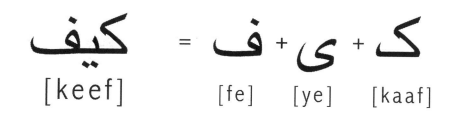

كـ + ى + ف = كيف

[kaaf] [ye] [fe] [keef]

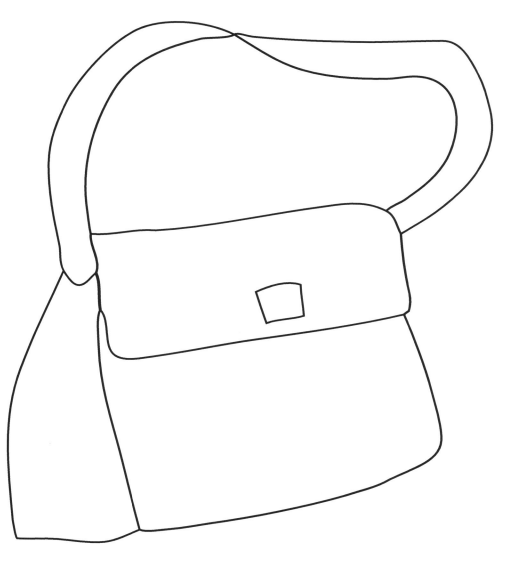

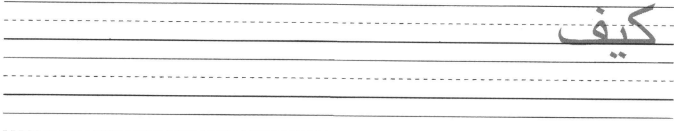

گ + و + ش = گوش

[goosh]   [sheen] [vaav] [gaaf]

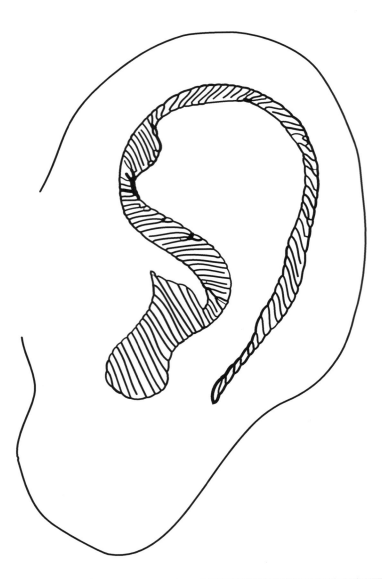

گَل = ل + گَ

[gul] [laam] [gaaf]

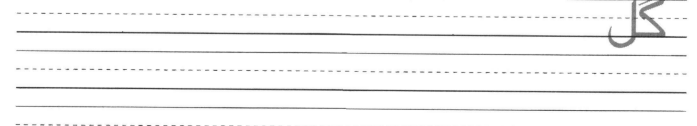

گَل

ل + ى + م + و = ليمو

[leemoo]   [vaav] [meem] [ye] [laam]

ليمو

ا + ن + ا + ر = انار

[anaar] [re] [alef] [noon] [alef]

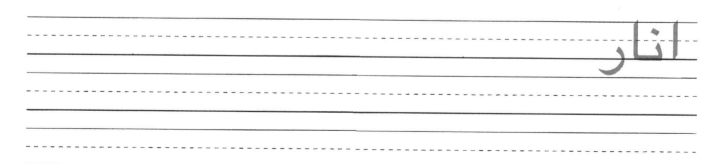

انار

ا + س + ب = اسب

[be] [seen] [alef]   [asb]

اسب

ا + ل + و = الو

[aloo]   [vaav] [laam] [alef]

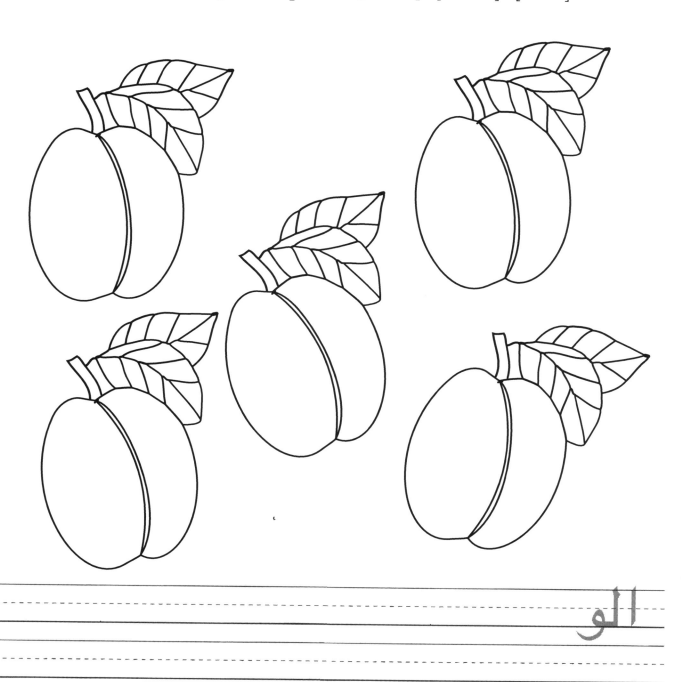

الو

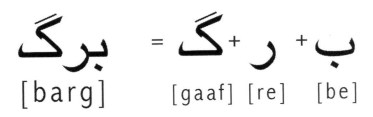

ب + ر + گ = برگ

[be] [re] [gaaf]   [barg]

برگ

پ + و + ل = پول

[pool]   [laam] [vaav] [pe]

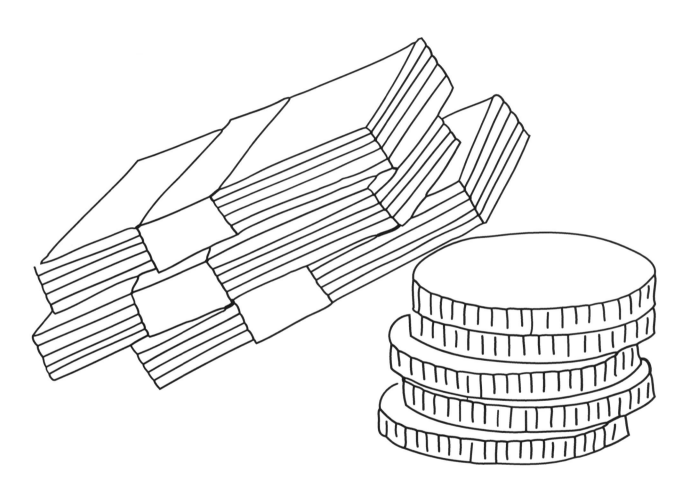

پول

ت + و + پ = توپ

[toop] [pe] [vaav] [te]

توپ

ت + و + ت   =   توت
[te] [vaav] [te]   [toot]

توت

ى + ا + س = ياس

[ye] [alef] [seen]   [yaas]

ياس

ت + ا + ر = تار

[te] [alef] [re]   [taar]

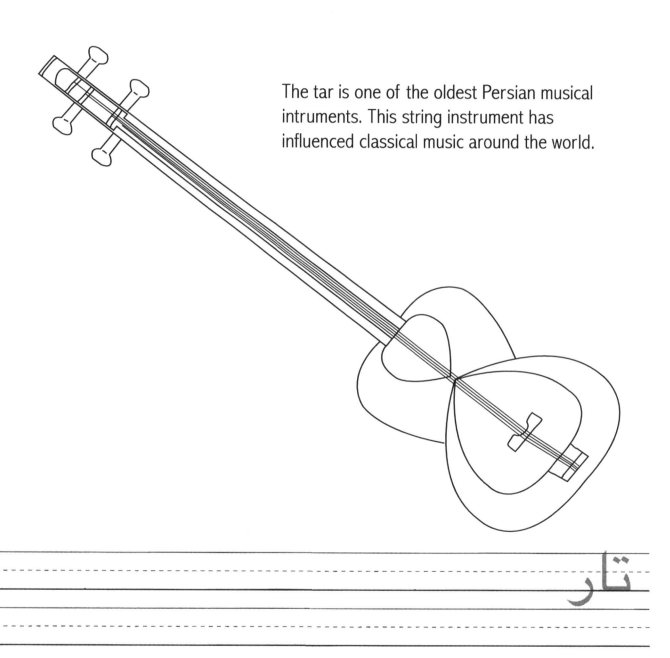

The tar is one of the oldest Persian musical intruments. This string instrument has influenced classical music around the world.

تار

نان = ن + ا + ن

[naan] = **[noon] [alef] [noon]**

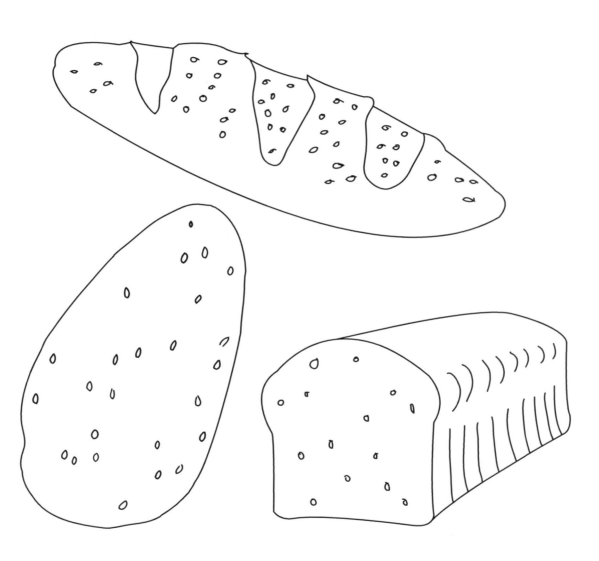

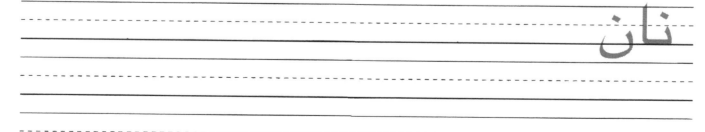

نان

ب + ا + غ = باغ

[be] [alef] [ghayn]   [baagh]

باغ

ب + ا + ل = بال

[be] [alef] [laam] [baal]

بال

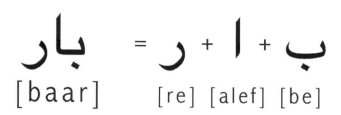

ب + ا + ر = بار

[baar] [re] [alef] [be]

بار

ب + ا + ب + ا = بابا

[be] [alef] [be] [alef]   [baabaa]

بابا

پا = ا + پ

[paa]   [alef] [pe]

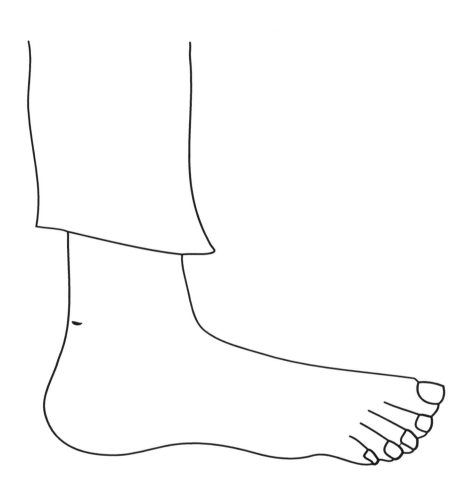

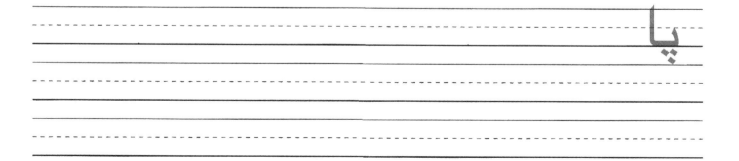

پَا

Now let's see how
letters join together
to make words!

ا + ب = اب

[alef] [be]   [aab]

اب

There are 7 letters that never join the letter after it (to their left). These letters never lose their tails.

ا

ـــــــ

ذ ‍د

ــــــــ ‍‍ ــــــــ

ژ ز ر

ــــــــ ــــــــ ــــــــ

و

ــــــــ

What are the names of these letters?

Draw a line between the matching letter shapes.

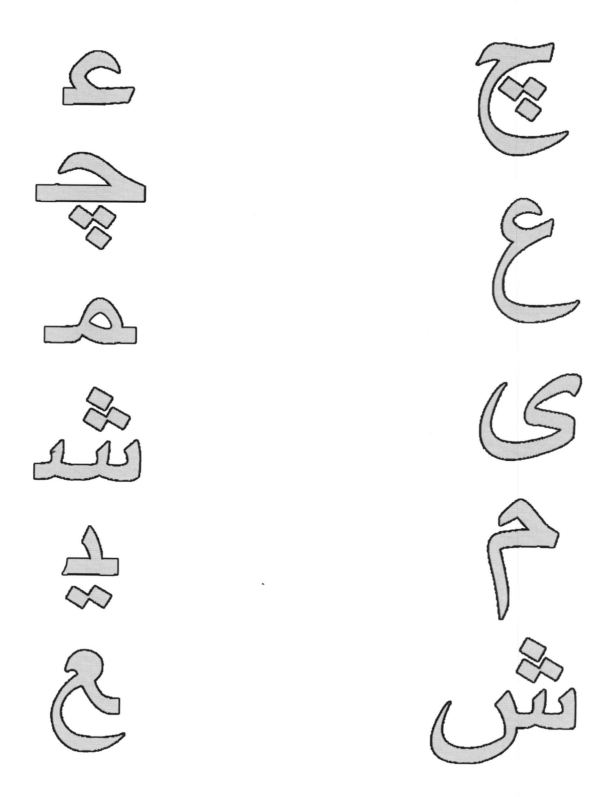

Draw a line between the matching letter shapes.

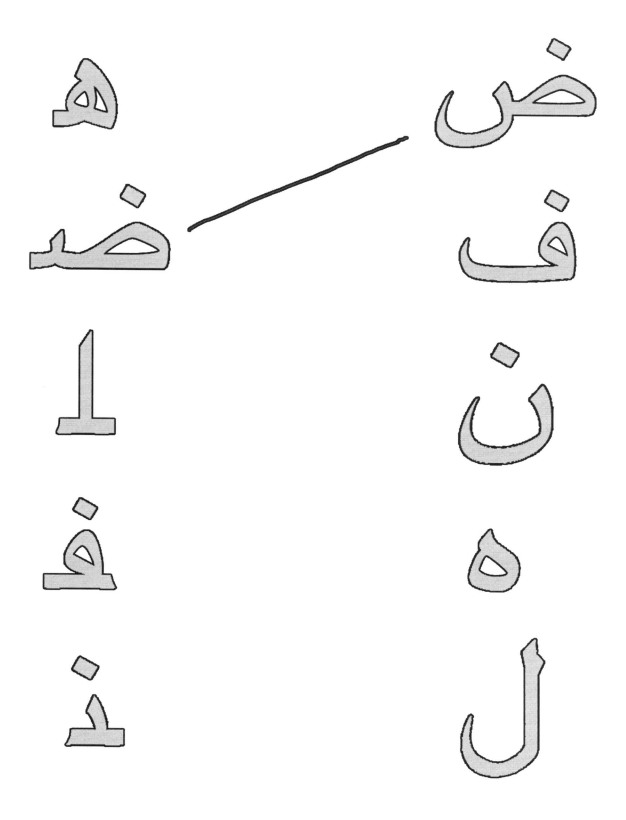

"He" is an example of a letter that completely changes its shape depending on where it is in a word.

ﻚ ﻪ ﻬ ﻩ

The letter "meem" has these shapes: ﻢ ﻤ م

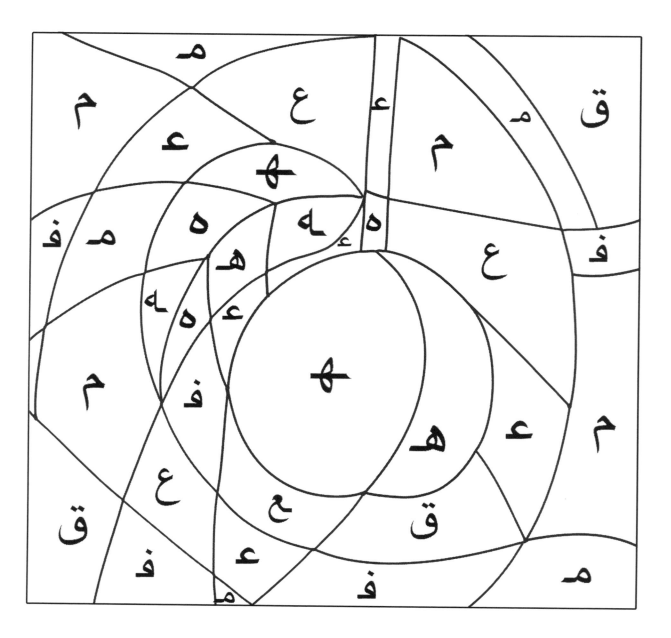

In this picture, color in all of the shapes with ﻚ, ﻪ, ﻬ, or ﻩ.

What are the names of these letters? Can you see how their shapes are different?

ف فـ ـفـ ـف — —   ع ـع ـعـ عـ — —

ق قـ ـقـ ـق — —   غ ـغ ـغـ غـ — —

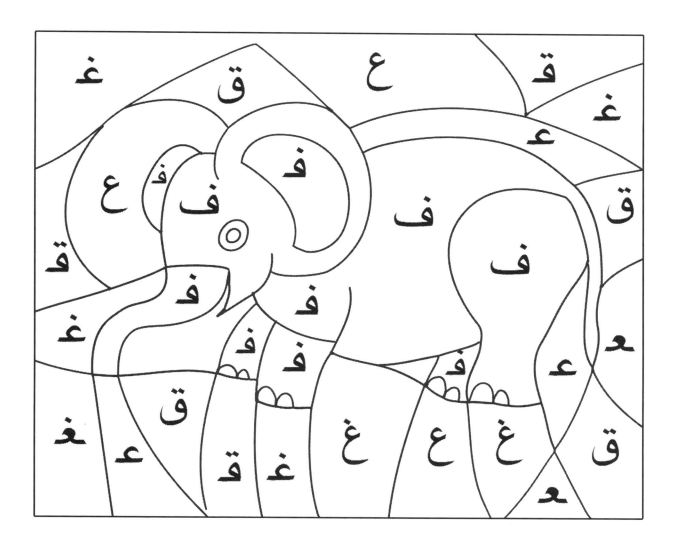

In this picture, color in all of the shapes with فـ ـفـ or ـف .

Do you remember the names of these letters? What happens when they lose their tail?

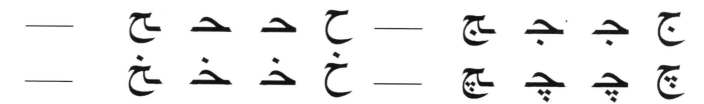

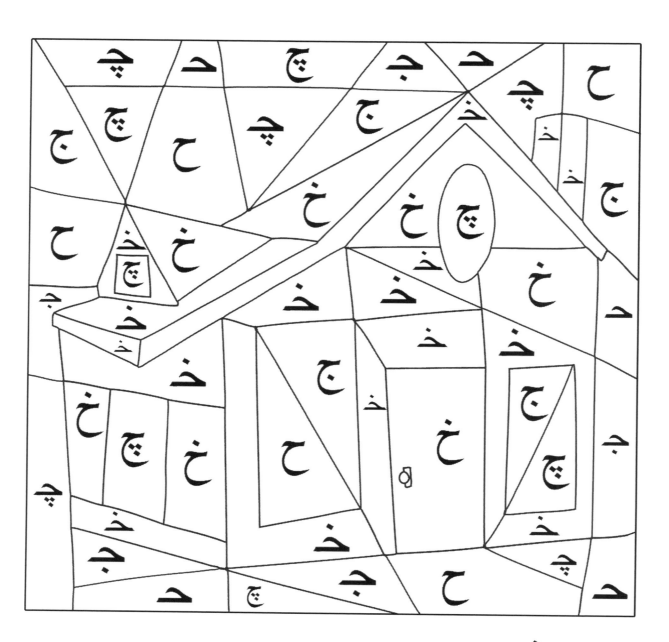

In this picture, color in all of the shapes with ﺧ or ﺥ.

These letters can also lose their tails. Can you see how they are similar and different?

—— ‫ص‬ ‫صـ‬ ‫صـ‬ ‫ص‬ ‫صـ‬ —— ‫سـ‬ ‫سـ‬ ‫سـ‬ ‫سـ‬ ‫س‬

—— ‫ض‬ ‫ضـ‬ ‫ضـ‬ ‫ض‬ ‫ضـ‬ —— ‫ش‬ ‫شـ‬ ‫شـ‬ ‫شـ‬ ‫ش‬

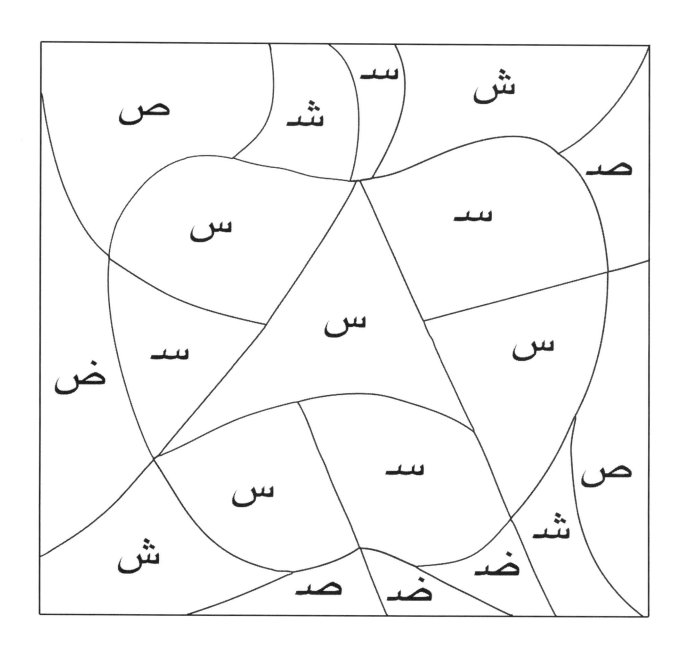

In this picture, color in all of the shapes with ‫سـ‬ or ‫س‬.

These letters lose their tails and change shape when they connect with other letters.
Can you see how these letters are similar and different from each other?

	ث	ثـ	ـثـ	ـث	ث		be	بـ	ـبـ	ـب	ب
	ن	نـ	ـنـ	ـن	ن			پـ	ـپـ	ـپ	پ
	ى	يـ	ـيـ	ـي	ى			تـ	ـتـ	ـت	ت

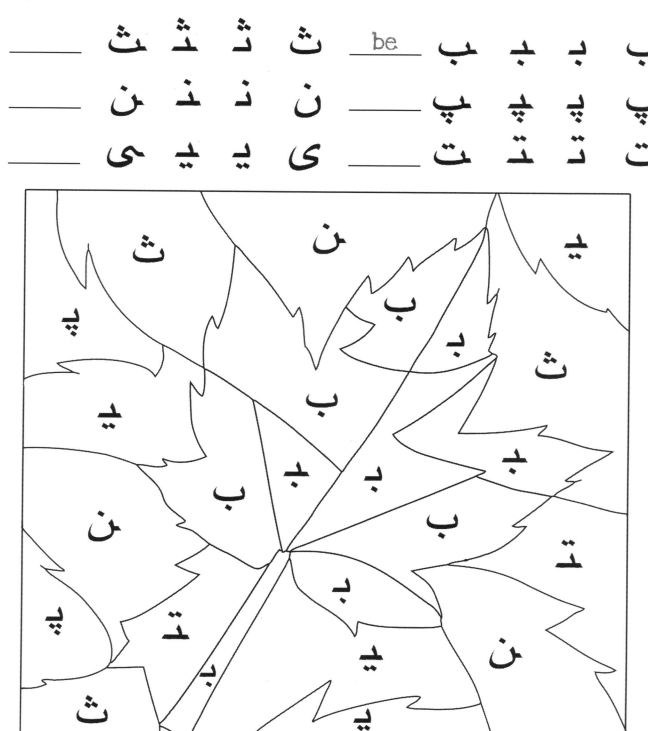

In this picture, color in all of the shapes with ـبـ , ـب , or ب .

Trace the letters of the alphabet and say the names of the letters out loud as you go. Remember to write from right to left. After you finish tracing, practice writing the letters in order on the lines below.

خ ح چ ج ث ت پ ب ا

ض ص ش س ژ ز ر ذ د

گ ک ق ف غ ع ظ ط

ی ه و ن م ل

Say the names of the letters out loud as you connect the dots.

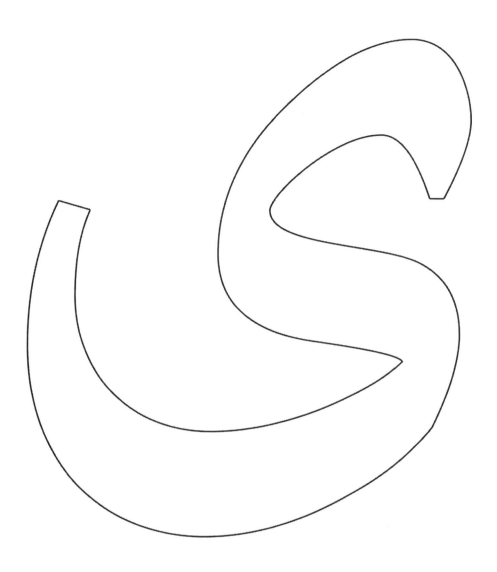

[ye]

Ɓ Ɓ Ɓ Ɓ Ɓ Ɓ Ɓ Ɓ Ɓ Ɓ Ɓ

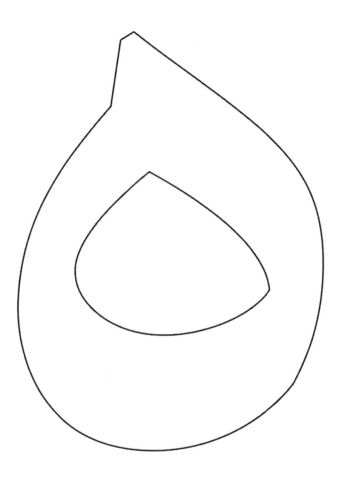

[he]

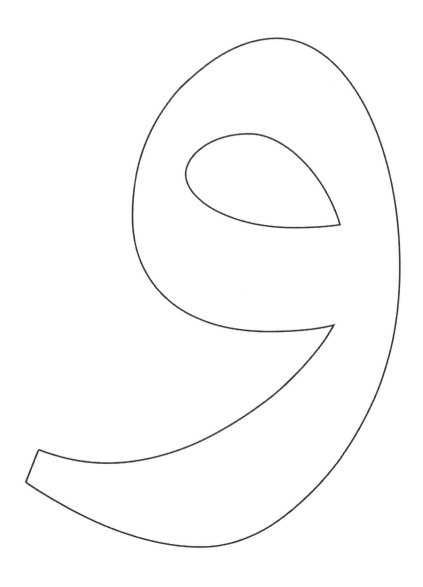

[vaav]

و و و و و و و و و و و و

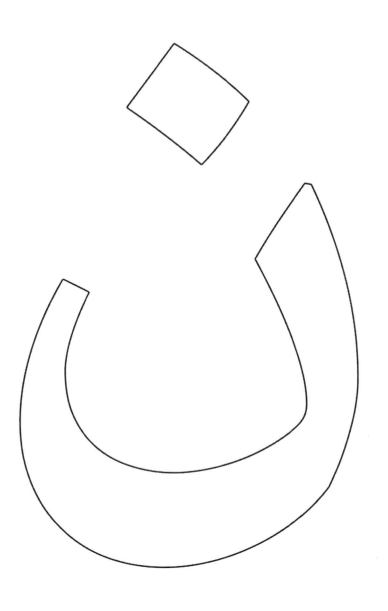

[noon]

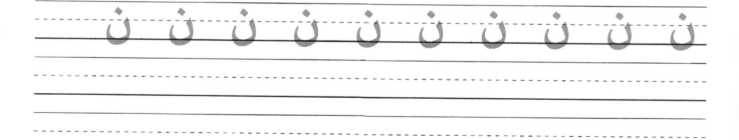

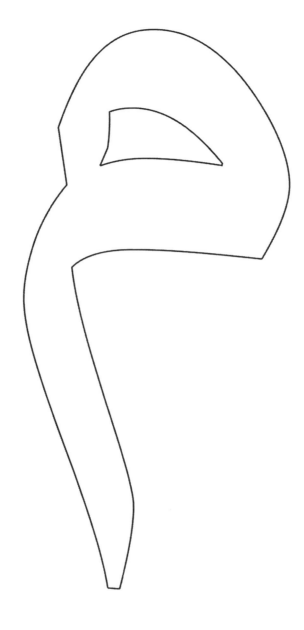

[meem]

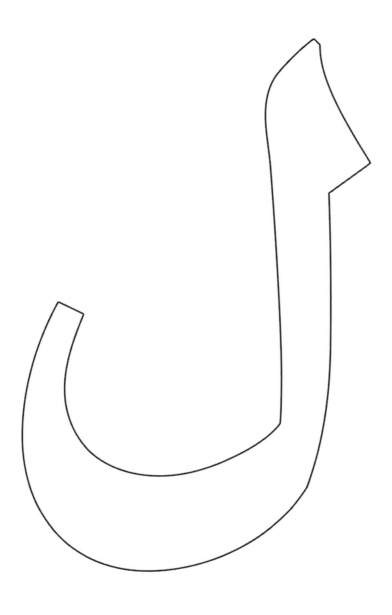

[laam]

[gaaf]

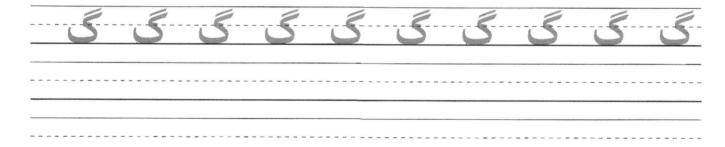

[kaaf]

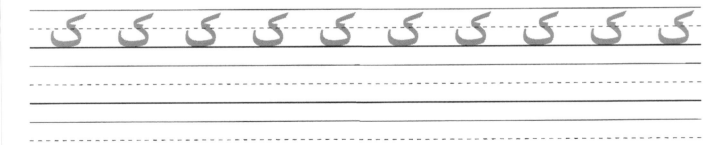

[ghaaf]

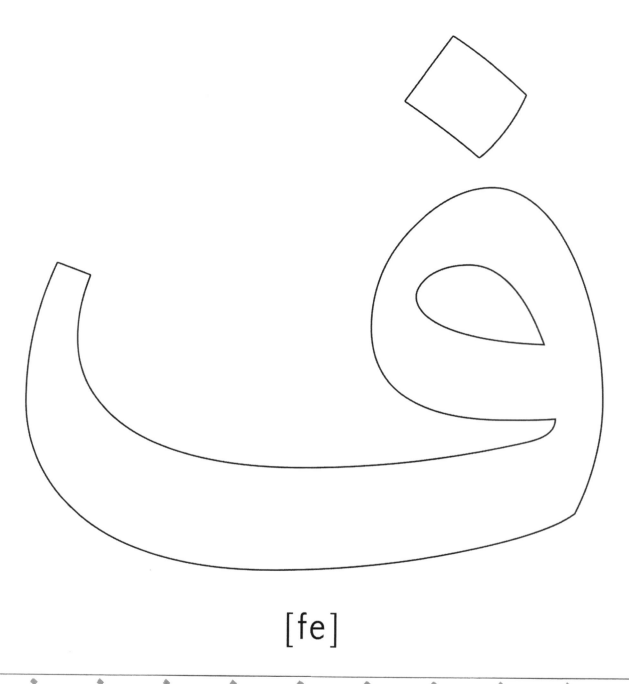

[fe]

ف ف ف ف ف ف ف ف ف

[ghayn]

غ غ غ غ غ غ غ غ غ غ

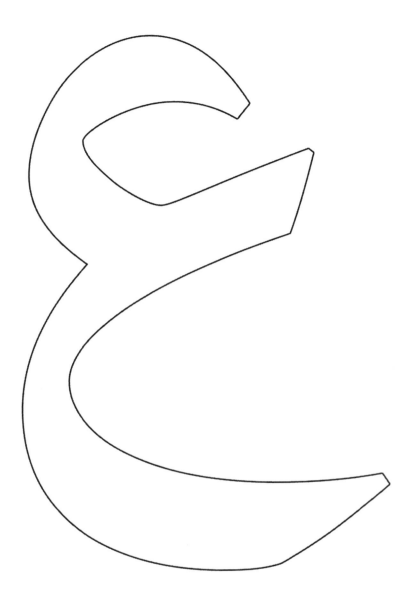

['ayn]

ع ع ع ع ع ع ع ع ع ع

Repeat the names of these Persian alphabet letters out loud
as you connect the dots in alphabetical order.

[zaa]

[taa]

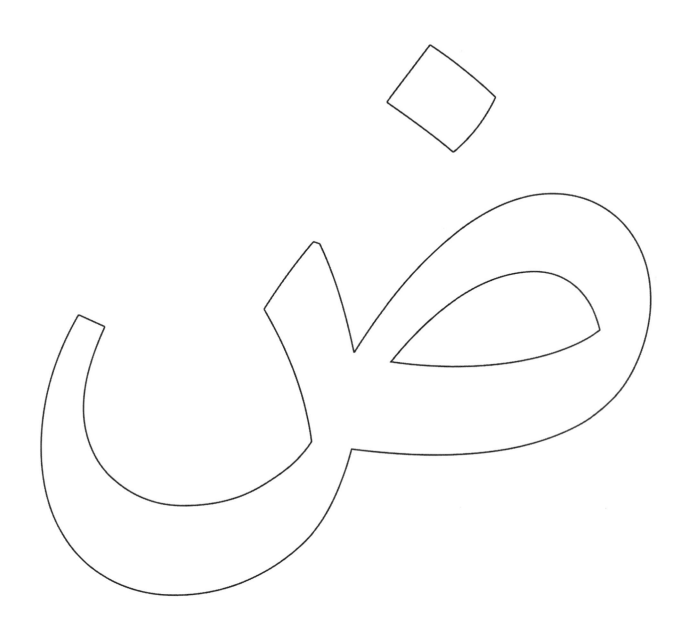

[zaad]

ض ض ض ض ض ض ض ض

[saad]

[sheen]

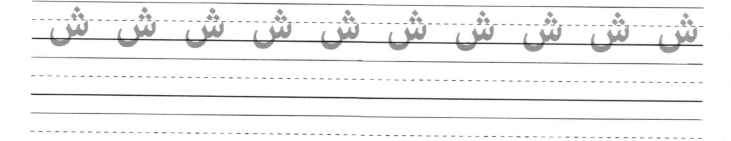

[seen]

ﺱ ﺱ ﺱ ﺱ ﺱ ﺱ ﺱ ﺱ ﺱ ﺱ ﺱ

Each dot below is labeled with a letter from the Persian alphabet.

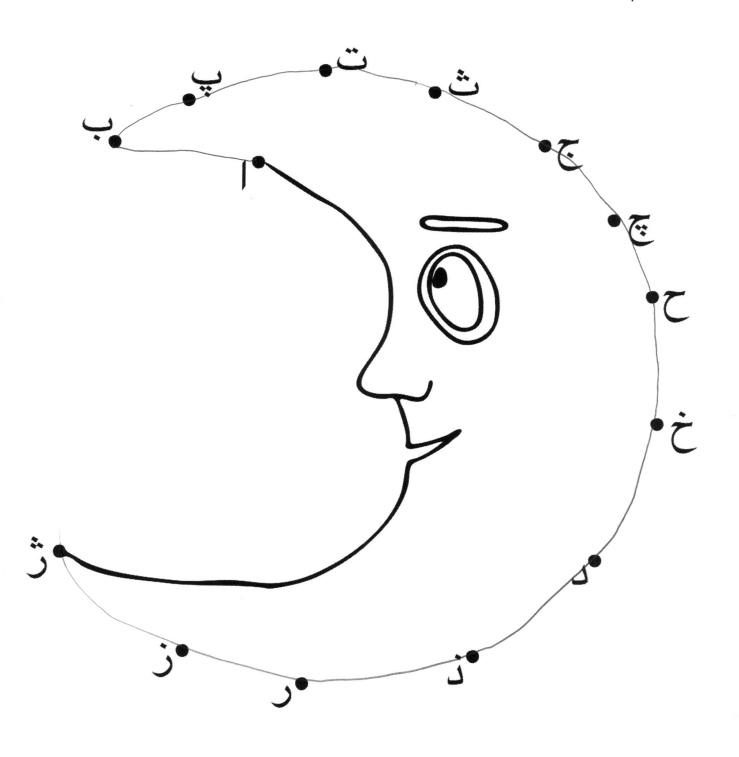

Connect the dots in alphabetical order.
Say the names of the letters out loud as you pass them.

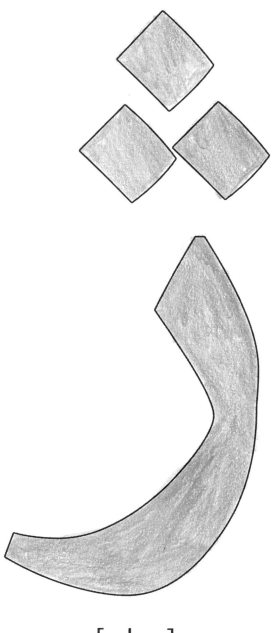

[zhe]

[ze]

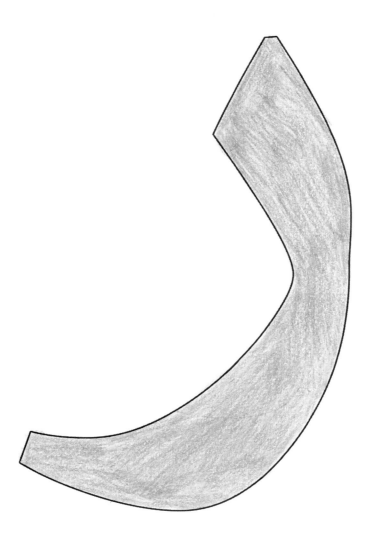

[re]

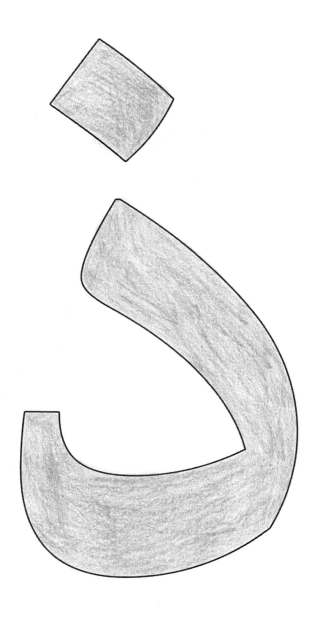

[zaal]

ذ ذ ذ ذ ذ ذ ذ ذ ذ ذ

ذ ذ ذ ذ ذ ذ ذ ذ ذ ذ

[daal]

[khe]

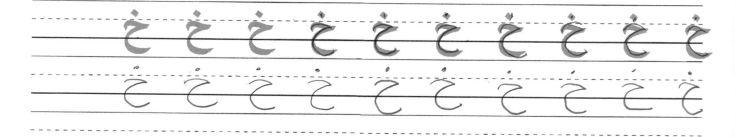

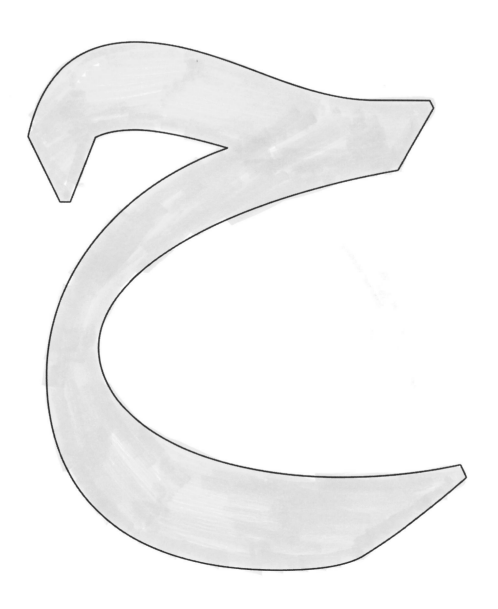

[he]

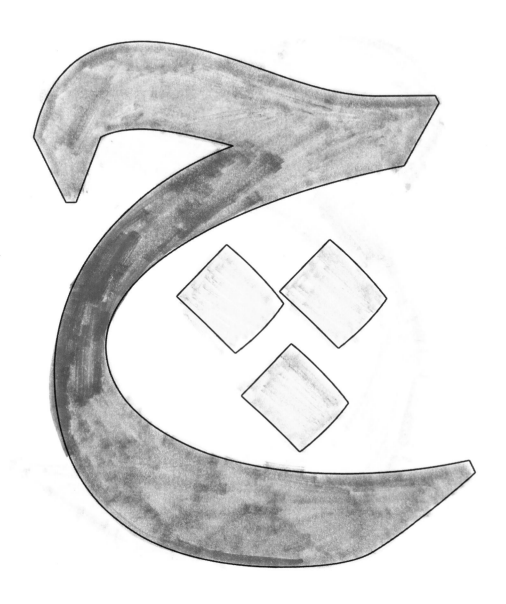

[che]

[jeem]

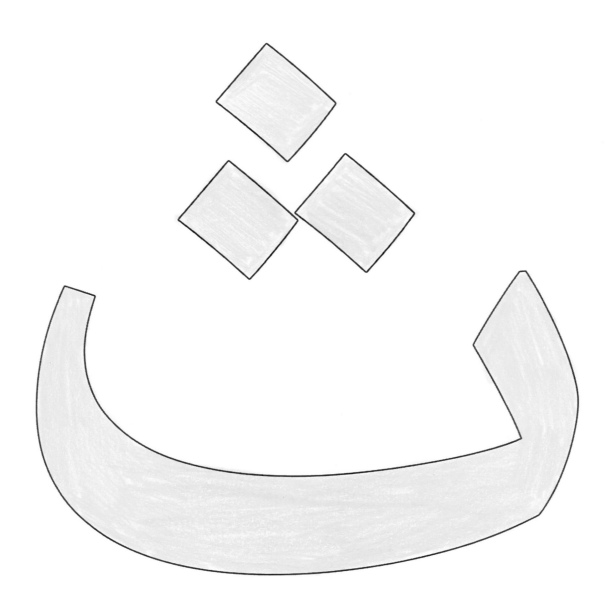

[se]

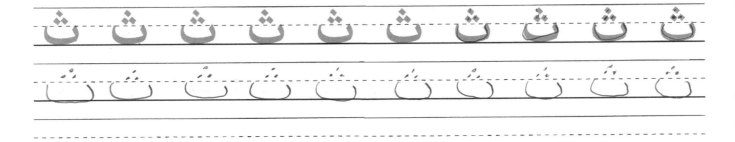

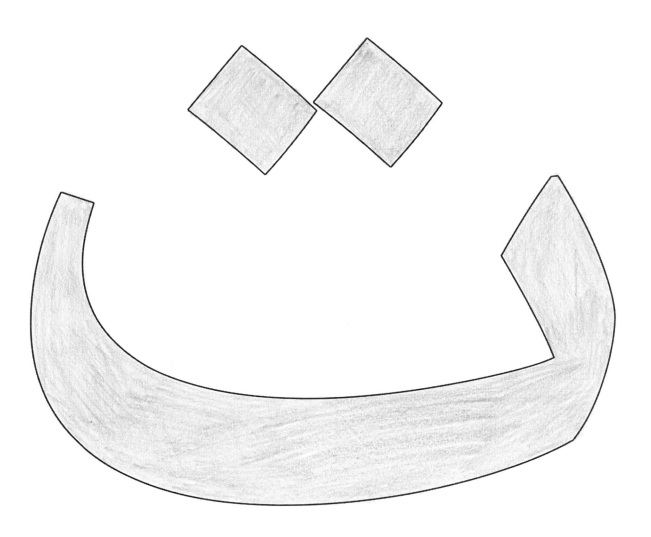

[te]

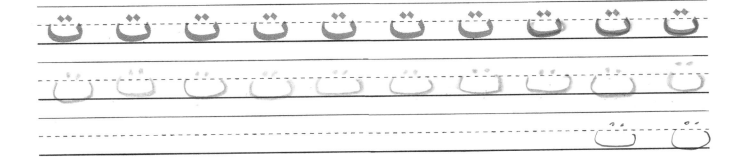

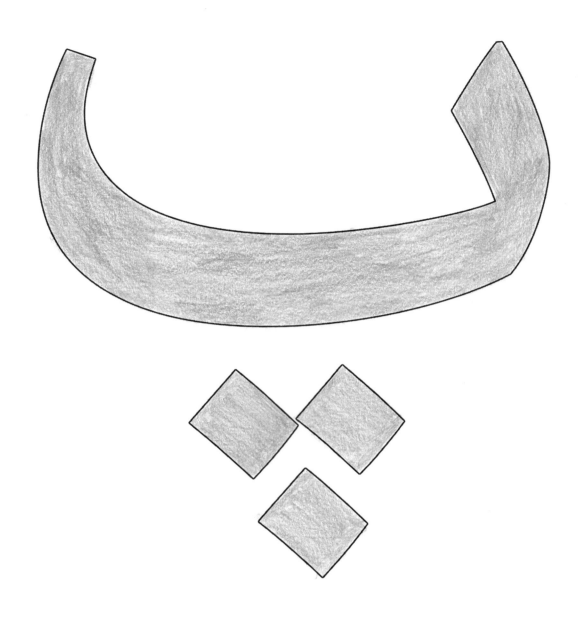

[pe]

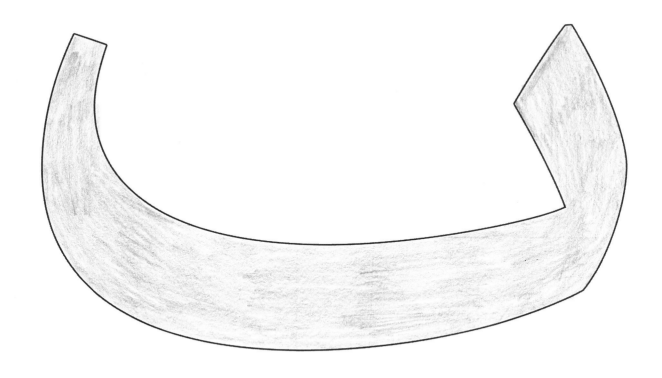

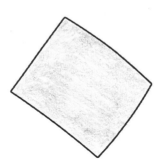

[be]

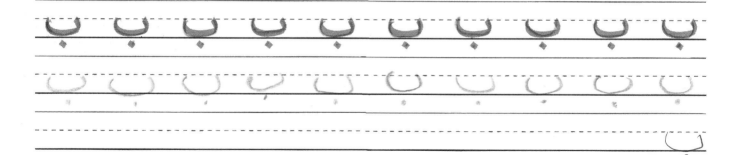

Color in each of the letters of the Persian alphabet. Say the name of each letter as you color. ➔

[alef]

Trace the letters here. Then try writing them on your own. ↓

The Persian Alphabet

الفبتای فارسی

ا
[alef]

ب
[be]

پ
[pe]

ت
[te]

ث
[se]

ج
[jeem]

چ
[che]

ح
[he]

خ
[khe]

د
[daal]

ذ
[zaal]

ر
[re]

ز
[ze]

ژ
[zhe]

س
[seen]

ش
[sheen]

ص
[saad]

ض
[zaad]

ط
[taa]

ظ
[zaa]

ع
['ayn]

غ
[ghayn]

ف
[fe]

ق
[ghaaf]

ک
[kaaf]

گ
[gaaf]

ل
[laam]

م
[meem]

ن
[noon]

و
[vaav]

ه
[he]

ی
[ye]

Hi! I'm Leila. I love learning new things.

Today I am going to begin learning the Persian alphabet and some words in Farsi, the Persian language. You can learn with me by doing the activities in this book.

In Farsi, reading and writing go right to left. That is why we are starting our activities from this side of the book. Turn the page to get started...

Made in the USA
Lexington, KY
06 January 2014